NO LONGER PROPERTY OF
SEATTLE PUBLIC LIBRARY

Cool Cookies & Bars

Easy Recipes for Kids to Bake

Pam Price

ABDO
Publishing Company

TO ADULT HELPERS

You're invited to assist up-and-coming pastry chefs in a kitchen near you! And it will pay off in many ways. Your children will develop new skills, gain confidence, and make some delicious treats while learning to bake. What's more, it's going to be a lot of fun.

These recipes are designed to let children bake independently as much as possible. Encourage them to do whatever they are able to do on their own. Also encourage them to try any variations supplied with the recipes and to experiment with their own ideas. Building creativity into the baking process encourages children to think like real chefs.

Before getting started, set some ground rules about using the kitchen, cooking tools, and ingredients. Most important, adult supervision is a must whenever a child uses the oven, stove, or sharp tools.

So put on your aprons and stand by. Let your young bakers take the lead. Watch and learn. Taste their creations. Praise their efforts. Enjoy the culinary adventure!

Visit us at www.abdopublishing.com

Published by ABDO Publishing Company, 8000 West 78th Street, Edina, Minnesota 55439. Copyright © 2010 by Abdo Consulting Group, Inc. International copyrights reserved in all countries. No part of this book may be reproduced in any form without written permission from the publisher. Checkerboard Library™ is a trademark and logo of ABDO Publishing Company.

Printed in the United States of America, North Mankato, Minnesota
092009
012010
PRINTED ON RECYCLED PAPER

Editor: Liz Salzmann
Series Concept: Nancy Tuminelly
Cover and Interior Design: Anders Hanson, Mighty Media, Inc.
Photo Credits: Anders Hanson, Brian McCarthy Photography (p. 29), Shutterstock

The following manufacturers/names appearing in this book are trademarks: Arm & Hammer®, C&H®, Kraft® Calumet®, Land O' Lakes®, Lunds® and Byerly's®, McCormick®, Morton®, Proctor Silex®, Roundy's®

Library of Congress Cataloging-in-Publication Data

Price, Pamela S.
Cool cookies & bars : easy recipes for kids to bake / Pam Price.
p. cm. -- (Cool baking)
Includes index.
ISBN 978-1-60453-775-8
1. Cookies--Juvenile literature. 2. Bars (Desserts)--Juvenile literature. I. Title.
TX772.P58 2010
641.8'654--dc22

2009025790

Table of Contents

BAKING IS COOL 4
READY, SET, BAKE! 5
SAFETY FIRST! 6
TOOLS OF THE TRADE 8
COOL INGREDIENTS 10
COOL TECHNIQUES 13
CLASSIC CHOCOLATE CHIP COOKIES 16
CHOCO-WAKKA COOKIES 18
SURPRISE MERINGUES 20
OATMEAL RAISIN COOKIES 22
SCRUMPTIOUS SAND TARTS 24
BODACIOUS BROWNIES 26
TERRIFIC TURTLE BARS 28
WRAP IT UP! 30
GLOSSARY 31
WEB SITES 31
INDEX 32

Baking Is Cool

Baking is like a fun chemistry experiment with delicious results!

If you stop to think about it, baking is like a chemistry experiment. You certainly wouldn't want to eat a handful of flour. But, if you mix flour with other ingredients and expose it to heat, you can transform the ingredients into something delicious. That's some tasty chemistry!

Baking depends on chemistry. You have to mix certain ingredients in a certain order. But baking also allows for creativity. The artistry comes in the flavors you add, the shapes you form, and the decorations you create.

So start rattling those cookie sheets and mixing bowls. You'll soon be baking wonderful treats to share with your family and friends.

GET THE PICTURE!

When a step number in a recipe has a colored circle around it, look for the picture that goes with it. The circle around the photo will be the same color as the step number.

Ready, Set, Bake!

Preparation is a key element of successful baking. Here are some things to keep in mind.

ASK PERMISSION

- Get permission to use the kitchen, baking tools, and ingredients.
- If you'd like to do something by yourself, say so. As long as you can do it safely, do it!
- Ask for help when you need it. Professional chefs have *sous chefs*, which means "assistant chefs" in French. You can have one too!

BE PREPARED

Read the whole recipe the day before you plan to bake.

- Make sure you have all the ingredients. Do you need to go to the grocery store?
- Will there be enough time? Sometimes dough needs to chill before you form it into cookies.

When it's time to bake, these steps will help you be organized.

- Gather all the tools and equipment you will need.
- Prepare the pans as directed and preheat the oven.
- Gather the listed ingredients. Sometimes you need prepared ingredients such as chopped nuts or sifted flour. Do those prep jobs as you gather the ingredients.
- Finally, do the recipe steps in the order they are listed.

Safety First!

When you bake you need to use an oven. Sometimes you also have to use sharp tools. Ask an adult helper to be in the kitchen with you. Here's how to keep it safe.

HOT STUFF

- Set up a cooling rack ahead of time.
- Make sure it's easy to get from the oven to the cooling area. There should be no people or things in the way.
- Always use oven mitts, not towels, when handling hot pots and pans.
- The oven is hot too. Don't bump into the racks or the door.

THAT'S SHARP

- Choose a small knife. Cut just a small amount of food at a time.
- Always keep your other hand away from the blade.
- Work slowly and keep your eyes on the knife.

KEY SYMBOLS

In this book, you will see some symbols beside the recipes. Here is what they mean.

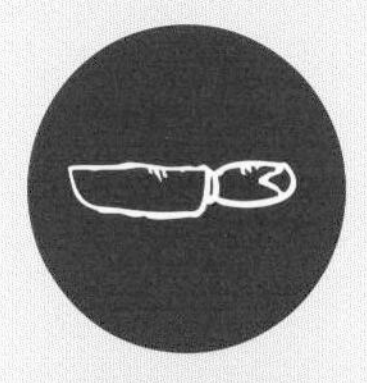

SUPER SHARP!

You need to use a knife for this recipe. Ask an adult to stand by.

SUPER COOL!

This symbol means there are other ways to make the recipe.

Germ Alert!

It's so tempting, but you shouldn't eat dough that contains raw eggs. Raw eggs may contain salmonella **bacteria**, which can cause food poisoning. Eating cookie dough that contains raw eggs might make you sick. Really sick! Ask an adult if it's okay to lick bowls, beaters, and spoons.

KEEP IT CLEAN

- Tie back long hair.
- Wash your hands before you begin baking. Rub them with soap for 20 seconds before rinsing. Wash them again if you eat, sneeze, cough, take a bathroom break, or touch the trash container.
- Use clean tools and equipment. If you lick a spoon, wash it before using it again.
- Make sure that your cutting board hasn't had raw meat on it.

Tools of the Trade

These are the basic tools used for baking cookies and bars.
Each recipe in this book lists the tools you will need.

MEASURING CUPS

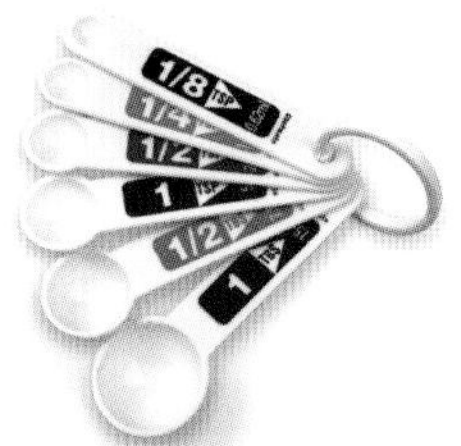

MEASURING SPOONS

KNIFE AND CUTTING BOARD

MIXING BOWLS

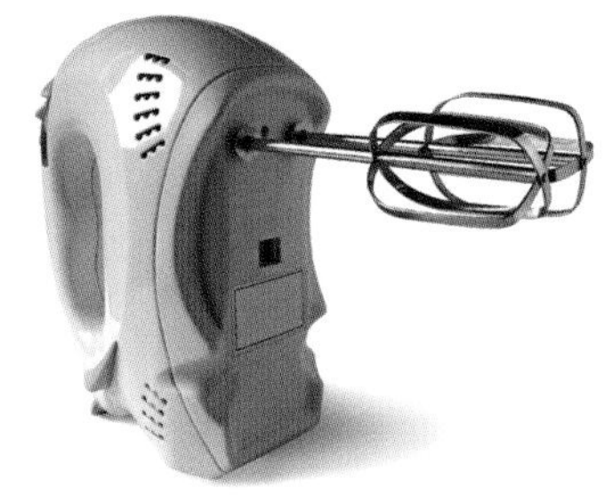

MIXER AND BEATERS

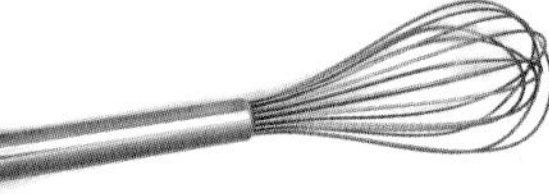

WHISK

SILICONE SPATULA

WOODEN SPOON

SIFTER

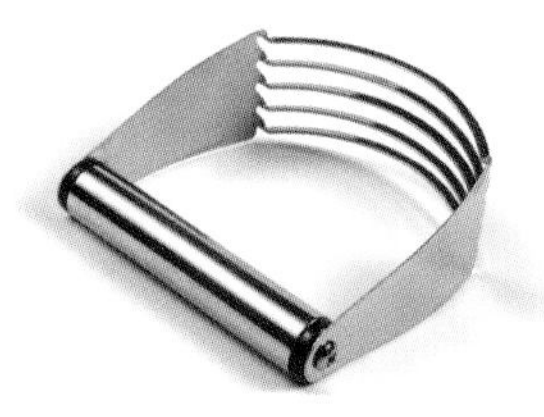

PASTRY BLENDER

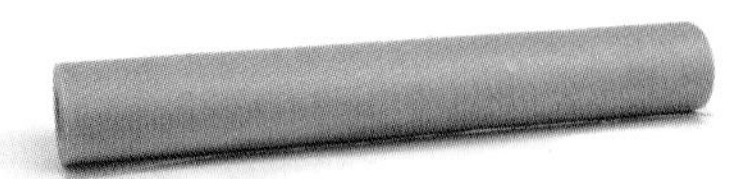

PARCHMENT PAPER

COOKIE SHEET

9 × 13-INCH PAN

8 × 8-INCH PAN

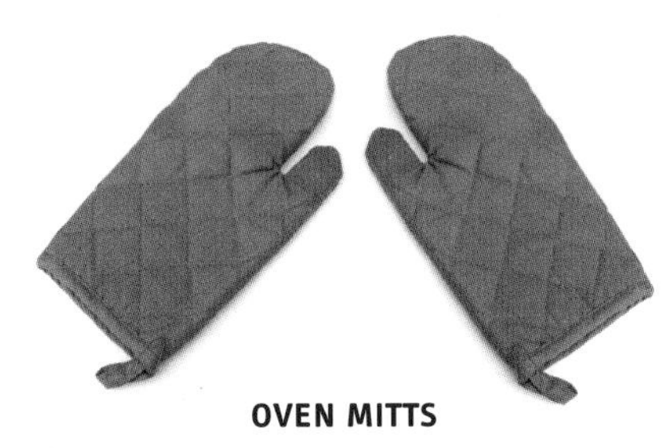
OVEN MITTS

Glass or Metal Pans?

Should you use glass or metal baking pans? Light-colored metal or dark-colored metal? The simple answer is to use whatever is available in your kitchen. But the material and the color do make a difference. Food bakes faster in glass and dark metal pans.

If you can, use a light-colored baking sheet for cookies. Cookies will brown more if they are baked on a dark-colored baking sheet.

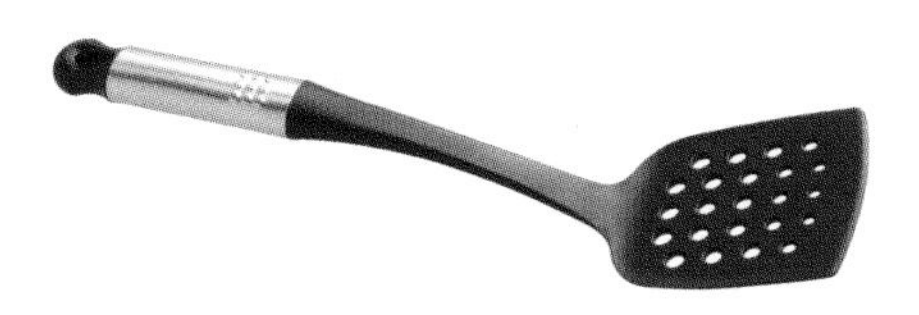
SPATULA

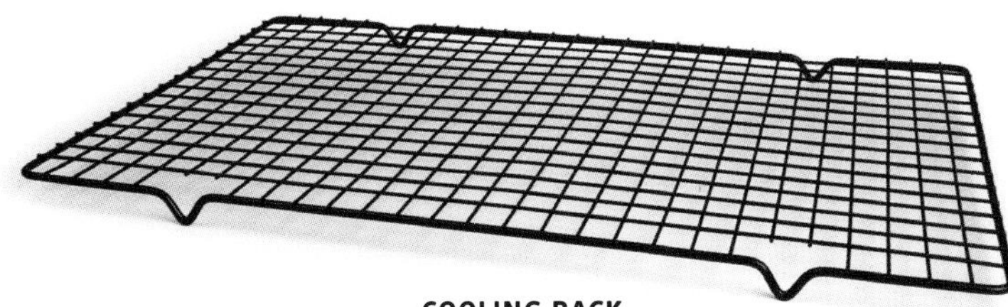
COOLING RACK

Cool Ingredients

Butter, flour, sugar. You can make many different goodies based on these three ingredients! Add a few others, and the possibilities are endless.

BUTTER

Choose unsalted butter for baking. You add salt in most recipes. Using unsalted butter keeps the dough from having too much salt.

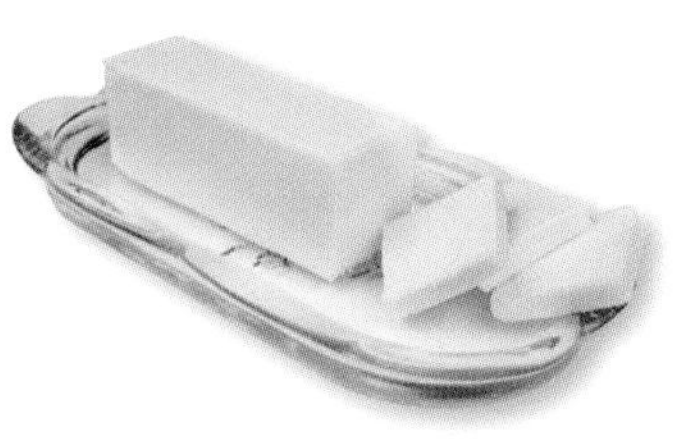

FLOUR

In a recipe, the word *flour* means all-purpose wheat flour. But other grains can be ground into flour too. Some of these grains include kamut, rye, buckwheat, and corn.

SUGAR

You use several types of sugar for baking. Most common are granulated sugar, powdered sugar, and brown sugar. Sometimes a recipe may call for corn syrup, molasses, or honey. If a recipe just says *sugar*, it means granulated sugar.

About Organics

Organic foods are grown without **synthetic** fertilizers and **pesticides.** This is good for the earth. And, recent studies show that organic foods may be more nutritious than **conventionally** grown foods.

Organic foods used to be hard to find. But now you can find organic versions of most foods. Organic foods are more expensive than conventionally grown foods. Families must decide for themselves whether to spend extra for organic foods.

EGGS

Eggs come in many sizes. Use large eggs unless the recipe says otherwise. Bring eggs to room temperature before you add them to the dough.

BAKING SODA AND BAKING POWDER

Baking soda and baking powder are common **leavening** agents. Leavening agents are ingredients that make baked goods rise.

SALT

You may be surprised to see salt in a dessert recipe. Salt is a flavor **enhancer**. It enhances the flavors in your baked goods, whether they are sweet or **savory**.

EXTRACTS

There are many flavoring **extracts** used in baking. Some of these are vanilla, lemon, and maple. You will probably use vanilla extract most often. Vanilla extract is made from the beans, or seedpods, of tropical orchids.

MILK AND CREAM

You can use whatever milk you have, whether it is skim, low fat, or whole milk. Substituting usually won't noticeably affect the quality of what you're making. However, use cream if a recipe says to.

Say What?

Older recipes may call for light cream or heavy cream. But those terms are not used much anymore. Use half-and-half if a recipe says light cream. Use heavy whipping cream if a recipe specifies heavy cream.

CHOCOLATE

Chocolate comes from the bean of the cacao tree. When cocoa beans are processed, the cocoa particles and the cocoa butter are separated. Then they are recombined in different **formulas** such as semisweet, bittersweet, and milk chocolate. In general, the higher the cocoa content, the stronger the taste.

Did You Know?

About 85 percent of cocoa beans are grown in Africa.

Ewww! What's that?

If it is warm or humid, chocolate may bloom. This means it develops a whitish powder on it. Don't worry. It's still okay to eat and to bake with.

NUTS

Nuts, usually walnuts or pecans, add flavor to baked goods. Luckily, you can buy them already sliced or chopped!

Allergy Alert

Millions of people have food allergies or food intolerance. Foods that most often cause allergic reactions include milk, eggs, peanuts, tree nuts, and wheat. Common food intolerances include lactose and gluten. Lactose is the sugar in milk. Gluten is the protein in wheat.

Baked goods can be a real hazard for people with food allergies or intolerances. If a friend cannot eat the goodies you're offering, don't be offended. It could be a life or death matter for your friend.

Cool Techniques

These are the techniques that bakers use. If you can't remember how to do something, just reread these pages.

MEASURING DRY INGREDIENTS

Dip the measuring spoon or measuring cup into whatever you're measuring. Use a butter knife to scrape off the excess.

MIXING DRY INGREDIENTS

Unless the recipe says otherwise, always stir the dry ingredients together first. Measure them into a bowl and stir them with a fork or a whisk.

CREAMING

Creaming means beating something until it is smooth and creamy. When baking, you often need to cream butter. Unless the recipe says otherwise, use butter that is near room temperature.

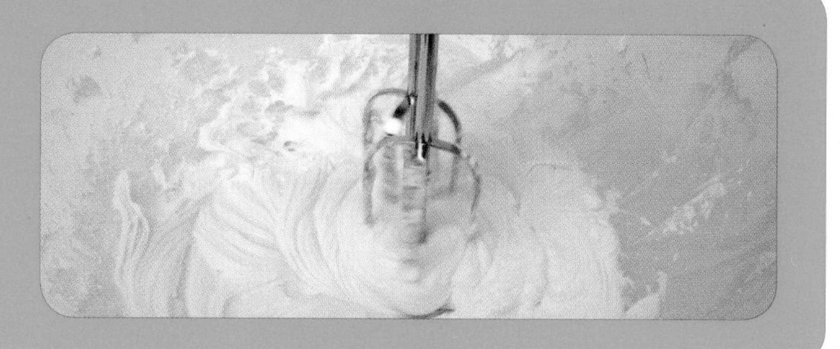

CUTTING IN

Cutting in means working butter into flour until the mixture is crumbly. Use a pastry blender, a fork, or your fingertips.

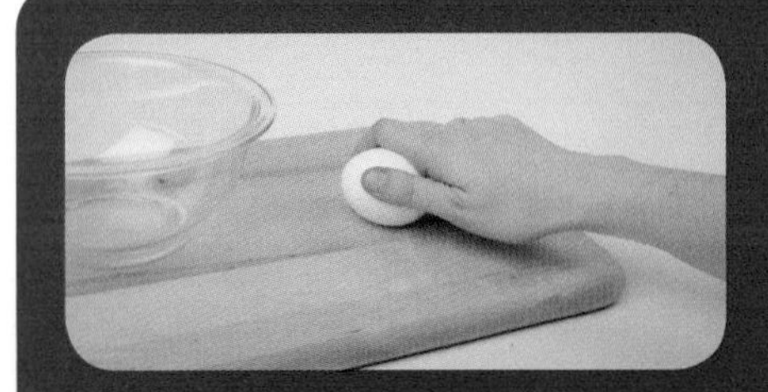

SEPARATING AN EGG

Rap the egg firmly on the countertop. Hold the egg over a bowl and pull the shell apart. Gently pass the egg back and forth between the pieces of shell. The white will fall into the bowl. The yolk will remain in the shell.

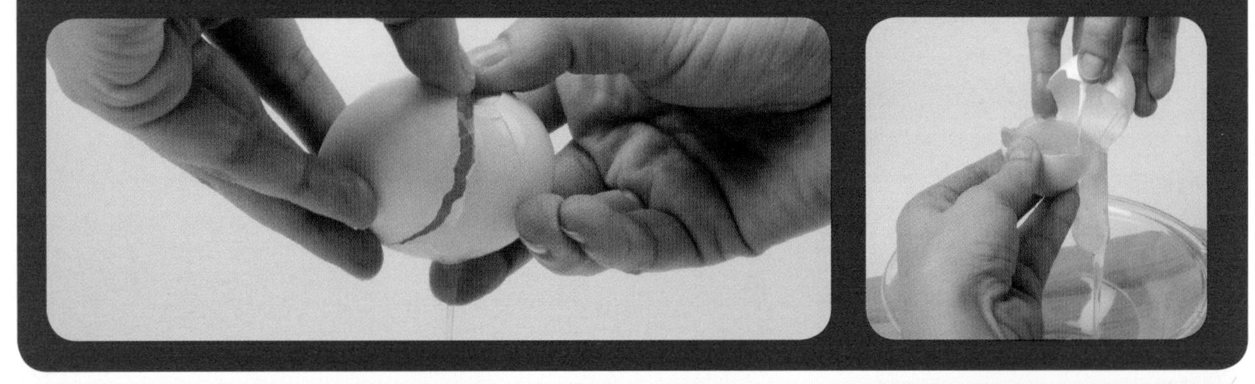

WHIPPING CREAM

Pour the whipping cream into a chilled bowl with deep sides. Beat on high speed until the cream forms peaks. Don't overbeat, or you will make butter!

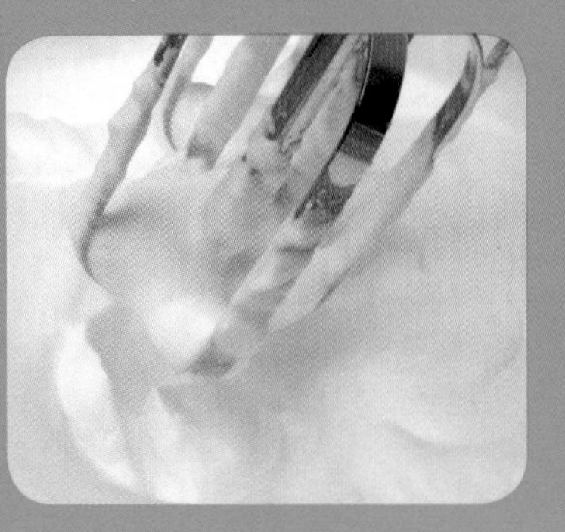

BEATING EGG WHITES

Egg whites won't get fluffy if there is fat, such as yolk, butter, or chocolate, in them. So, use a clean metal bowl and clean beaters. Make sure there is no yolk in the whites. Beat on high speed until the whites reach the desired firmness.

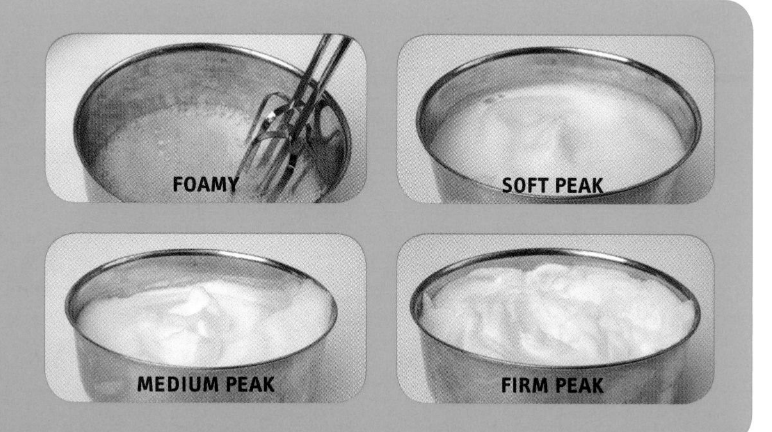

MELTING CHOCOLATE

To melt chocolate on the stove, use a double boiler. Put a little water in the bottom part. Put the chocolate in the top part. Turn the burner on low. Simmer the water until the chocolate melts. Stir often.

Word Order Counts!

Pay attention to word order in the ingredients list. If it says "1 cup sifted flour," that means you sift some flour and then measure it. If the list says "1 cup flour, sifted," that means you measure first and then sift. Believe it or not, this makes a difference. Sifted flour is fluffier than unsifted flour. This means less of it fits in the measuring cup.

GREASING A COOKIE SHEET

There are several ways to grease a cookie sheet. One is to wipe the pan with the butter wrapper. There's usually just enough butter left on it. You can also use a paper towel to rub butter on the pan. Or you can line it with parchment paper or a silicone mat.

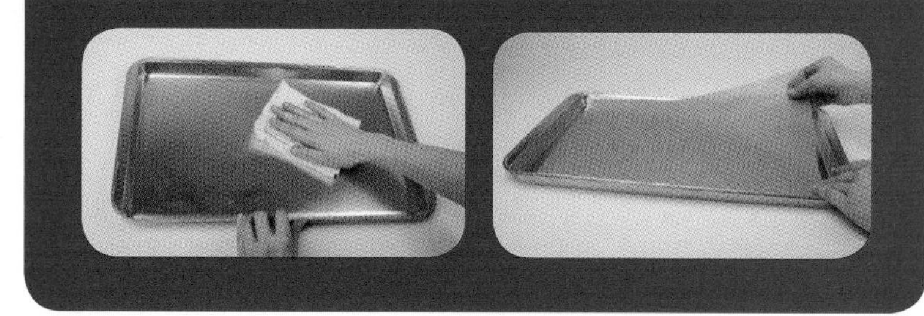

Classic Chocolate Chip Cookies

A warm chocolate chip cookie with a glass of cold milk can't be beat!

MAKES ABOUT 3 DOZEN COOKIES

INGREDIENTS

- 1½ cups flour
- ½ teaspoon baking soda
- ½ teaspoon salt
- ⅔ cup butter, softened
- ½ cup sugar
- ½ cup packed brown sugar
- 1 egg
- 1 teaspoon vanilla extract
- 1 cup semisweet chocolate chips
- ½ cup chopped walnuts (optional)

TOOLS: mixing bowls, measuring cups, measuring spoons, whisk, mixer and beaters, silicone spatula, wooden spoon, dinner spoons, cookie sheets, cooling rack, oven mitts, spatula

1. Preheat the oven to 375 degrees.

2. Whisk together the flour, baking soda, and salt. Set this bowl aside for now.

3. In another mixing bowl, cream the butter and the sugars. The mixture should be light and fluffy.

4. Beat in the egg and the vanilla.

5. Gradually stir the dry ingredients into the butter mixture. Then stir in the chocolate chips and the walnuts.

6. Use two dinner spoons to drop dough onto an ungreased cookie sheet. Use one spoon to push the dough off the other. Space the cookies about 2 inches apart.

7. Bake for 8 to 10 minutes. Let the cookies cool on the pan for about a minute. Then transfer them to the cooling rack with a spatula.

Super Cool!

- Replace semisweet chocolate chips with M&Ms, milk chocolate chips, or peanut butter chips.
- Use white chocolate chips instead of semisweet chocolate chips. Use macadamia nuts instead of walnuts.
- Ask an adult helper to chop up Mexican chocolate, such as Ibarra. Use that instead of chocolate chips. Add 2 teaspoons cinnamon, ⅛ teaspoon ground black pepper, and ¼ teaspoon cayenne pepper when you add the vanilla. Now that's a spicy hot chocolate treat!

Choco-Wakka Cookies

Double the chocolate, double the goodness!

MAKES ABOUT 4 DOZEN COOKIES

INGREDIENTS

- 2 cups plus 2 tablespoons flour
- ¾ cup cocoa powder
- 1 teaspoon baking soda
- ½ teaspoon salt
- 1¼ cups butter, softened
- 2 cups sugar
- 2 eggs
- 1 tablespoon vanilla extract
- 12 ounces semisweet chocolate chips

TOOLS: mixing bowls, measuring cups, measuring spoons, whisk, mixer and beaters, silicone spatula, wooden spoon, dinner spoons, cookie sheets, spatula, cooling rack, oven mitts

1. Preheat the oven to 350 degrees.

2. Whisk together the flour, cocoa powder, baking soda, and salt. Set aside the dry ingredients.

3. Cream the butter and sugar until it is light and fluffy.

4. Beat in the eggs one at a time. Then beat in the vanilla.

5. Stir in the dry ingredients and then the chocolate chips.

6. Using dinner spoons, drop the cookie dough onto an ungreased cookie sheet. Space the cookies about 2 inches apart.

7. Bake for 8 to 10 minutes. Let the cookies cool on the pan for about 2 minutes. Then transfer them to the cooling rack with a spatula.

Surprise Meringues

MAKES ABOUT
2 DOZEN COOKIES

Chocolate chips and walnuts hide inside these cookies!

INGREDIENTS

- 2 egg whites at room temperature
- 1/8 teaspoon cream of tartar
- 1/2 teaspoon salt
- 1 teaspoon vanilla extract
- 3/4 cup sugar
- 1 cup semisweet chocolate chips
- 1/2 cup chopped walnuts (optional)

TOOLS: mixing bowls, parchment paper, cookie sheets, mixer and beaters, silicone spatula, measuring spoons, measuring cups, dinner spoons, oven mitts, spatula

1. Preheat the oven to 300 degrees. Line the cookie sheets with parchment paper. Or you can cut up brown paper bags to use instead.

2. Put the egg whites, cream of tartar, and salt in a bowl. Whip until soft peaks form. Then beat in the vanilla.

3. Continue beating the egg mixture while gradually adding the sugar.

4. Stir in the chocolate chips and the walnuts.

5. Drop spoonfuls of the batter onto the paper-lined cookie sheets. Space them about 2 inches apart.

6. Bake for 25 minutes.

7. Leave the cookies on the paper until they are completely cool. Then carefully peel them from the paper.

Oatmeal Raisin Cookies

These are so good that everyone will sit next to you at lunch, hoping you have an extra!

MAKES ABOUT
5 DOZEN COOKIES

INGREDIENTS

- 2 cups flour
- 1 teaspoon baking powder
- 1 teaspoon baking soda
- ½ teaspoon salt
- 1 teaspoon cinnamon
- ¼ teaspoon nutmeg
- 1⅓ cups butter
- 2 cups packed brown sugar
- ⅔ cup sugar
- 2 eggs
- 1 tablespoon vanilla extract
- 4 cups quick-cooking oats
- 1 cup raisins
- 2 tablespoons sugar for topping

TOOLS: cookie sheets, mixing bowls, measuring cups, measuring spoons, whisk, mixer and beaters, wooden spoon, dinner spoons, saucer, drinking glass, spatula, cooling rack, oven mitts

1. Preheat the oven to 350 degrees. Grease the cookie sheets.

2. Whisk together the flour, baking powder, baking soda, salt, cinnamon, and nutmeg. Set aside the bowl for now.

3. Cream the butter on medium speed. Add the sugars. Beat until the mixture is fluffy and light.

4. Beat in the eggs and the vanilla.

5. Stir in flour mixture.

6. Stir in the oats and the raisins.

7. Roll the dough into 1½-inch balls. Place them on the cookie sheets about 3 inches apart.

8. Pour 2 tablespoons of sugar into a saucer. Grease the bottom of the drinking glass. Dip the bottom of the glass in the sugar. Flatten a ball of dough with the bottom of the glass. Repeat until all the balls of dough are flattened.

9. Bake for 8 to 10 minutes. Let the cookies cool on the pan for about 2 minutes. Then transfer them to the cooling rack with a spatula.

Scrumptious Sand Tarts

These buttery cookies seem to melt in your mouth!

MAKES ABOUT 4 DOZEN COOKIES

INGREDIENTS

1 cup butter

½ cup powdered sugar, plus some extra

1 teaspoon vanilla extract

2 cups flour

1 cup chopped pecans

TOOLS:

mixing bowl
knife
cutting board
measuring cups
measuring spoons
mixer and beaters
silicone spatula
cookie sheets
spatula
cooling rack
oven mitts
sifter

Preheat the oven to 325 degrees.

2

Cream the butter. Then beat in the ½ cup of powdered sugar and the vanilla.

Stir in the flour and the nuts.

Roll the dough into 1-inch balls. Place them about 1 inch apart on an ungreased cookie sheet. Gently flatten them into disks.

Bake for 22 to 25 minutes. Let the cookies cool on the pan for about 2 minutes. Then transfer them to the cooling rack with a spatula. While the cookies are still warm, sift a light coating of powdered sugar over them.

Super Cool!

Don't sprinkle the cookies with powdered sugar. Instead, let them cool completely. Then melt 6 ounces of chocolate chips in a double boiler. Dip each cookie halfway into the melted chocolate. Place the cookies on waxed paper until the chocolate hardens.

Bodacious Brownies

These brownies are pure fudgy goodness!

MAKES 9 BROWNIES

INGREDIENTS

- 6 ounces bittersweet chocolate (not unsweetened)
- ½ cup butter
- 2 eggs
- 1 cup sugar
- 1 tablespoon cocoa powder
- 1 teaspoon vanilla extract
- 1 teaspoon cinnamon
- ½ teaspoon salt
- 1 cup flour

TOOLS: 8 × 8-inch baking pan, aluminum foil, saucepan, mixing bowl, wooden spoon, silicone spatula, toothpick, cooling rack, oven mitts, knife

Preheat the oven to 350 degrees. Line the baking pan with aluminum foil. Grease the foil.

2

Put the chocolate and the butter in the saucepan. Heat, stirring often, on medium-low until the butter and chocolate are melted. Remove the pan from the heat. Let the mixture cool to room temperature.

3

Put the chocolate mixture in a mixing bowl. Add the eggs, sugar, cocoa powder, vanilla, cinnamon, and salt. Stir just until mixed.

Stir in the flour.

5

Pour the batter into the prepared pan. Use a silicone spatula to spread the batter evenly. Bake for about 25 to 30 minutes. It's done when a toothpick stuck in the center comes out clean. Place the pan on a cooling rack until the brownies cool completely.

6

Use the edges of the foil to lift the brownies from the pan. Cut them into squares.

Terrific Turtle Bars

MAKES ABOUT
32 BARS

Turtle bars taste terrific and are terrifically easy to make!

INGREDIENTS

FOR THE CRUST LAYER

2 cups flour

1 cup packed brown sugar

½ cup plus 2 tablespoons butter, softened

1½ cups pecan halves

FOR THE CARAMEL LAYER

⅔ cup butter

½ cup packed brown sugar

FOR THE TOPPING

12 ounces semisweet chocolate chips

TOOLS: mixing bowl, pastry blender, 9 × 13-inch baking dish, saucepan, silicone spatula, cooling rack, oven mitts, knife

1 Preheat the oven to 350 degrees.

2 Stir together the flour and the brown sugar. Cut in the butter until the mixture resembles fine crumbs.

3 Pour this mixture into the baking dish. Pat it down evenly.

4 Sprinkle the pecan halves evenly over the crust.

5 Now make the caramel layer. Put the butter and the brown sugar in the saucepan. Cook over medium heat, stirring constantly, until the entire surface bubbles.

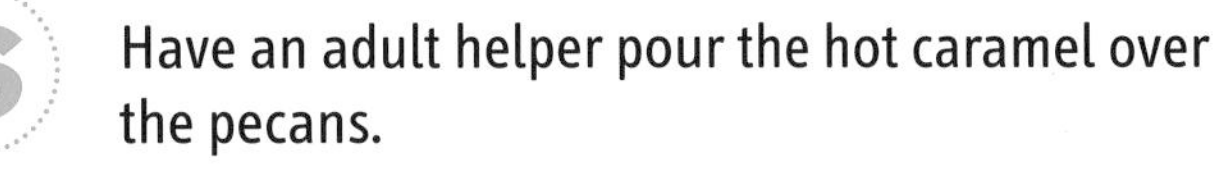

6 Have an adult helper pour the hot caramel over the pecans.

7 Bake for 18 to 22 minutes. The entire surface of the caramel should be bubbling.

8 Place the pan on a cooling rack. After 5 minutes, sprinkle the chocolate chips over the caramel layer. When the chocolate has melted, spread it over the entire surface. Cool completely before cutting the bars.

Wrap It Up!

Tips for keeping the treats you make fresh and delicious!

To store cookies, put them in an airtight container. Plastic food savers and plastic zipper bags are great for this.

You can also freeze cookies. Put them in a freezer bag before putting them in the freezer. Take out a couple in the morning. They'll be thawed in time for lunch or an afterschool snack!

Homemade cookies make great gifts. You can share them with your friends and family. You can give them to neighbors. You can give them to your teacher as a thank-you gift. Just put them in a pretty basket or box. Line the basket or box with colorful, food-safe tissue paper.

Glossary

bacteria – tiny, one-celled organisms that can only be seen through a microscope.

bodacious – remarkable or extraordinary.

conventional – in the usual way.

enhance – to increase or improve.

extract – a product made by concentrating the juices taken from something such as a plant.

formula – a combination of specific amounts of different ingredients or elements.

germ – a tiny, living organism that can make people sick.

leavening – a substance such as yeast or baking soda that makes baked goods rise.

pesticide – a substance used to kill insects.

savory – tasty and flavorful but not sweet.

scrumptious – delicious and excellent.

synthetic – produced artificially through chemistry.

Web Sites

To learn more about cool baking, visit ABDO Publishing Company on the World Wide Web at **www.abdopublishing.com.** Web sites about cool baking are featured on our Book Links page. These links are routinely monitored and updated to provide the most current information available.

Index

A

Adult help (for safety), 5, 6, 7, 17. *See also* Safety
Allergies (to foods), 12

B

Baking powder, 11
Baking soda, 11
Beating egg whites, 15
Brownies, 26–27
Butter, 10, 13, 14, 15
Butter cookies, 24–25

C

Chemistry (and baking), 4
Chocolate, 12, 15, 17, 25
Chocolate chip cookies, 16–17
Chocolate cookies, 18–19
Cleanliness, 7
Cookie sheets (greasing of), 15. *See also* Pans
Cream, 11, 14
Creaming, 13
Creativity (and baking), 4
Cutting in, 14

E

Eggs, 7, 11, 14, 15
Extracts, 11

F

Flour, 10, 14
Freezing (of cookies), 30

G

Germs, 7
Gifts (of cookies), 30
Greasing (of cookie sheets), 15

I

Ingredients, 10–12
 buying, 5
 list of in recipe, 5, 15
 preparing, 5
 types of, 10–12

K

Knife use, 6, 7, 17

M

Measuring dry ingredients, 13
Melting chocolate, 15
Meringues, 20–21
Milk, 11
Mixing dry ingredients, 13

N

Nuts, 12

O

Oatmeal raisin cookies, 22–23
Organic food, 10
Oven use, 6

P

Pans (for baking), 9, 15
Permission (for kitchen use), 5
Preparation (for baking), 5

R

Recipes (following directions in), 5, 15

S

Safety, 6–7
 adult help for, 5, 6, 7, 17
 allergies and, 12
 cleanliness and, 7
 guidelines for, 6–7
 knife use and, 6, 7, 17
 oven use and, 6
Salt, 11
Sand tarts, 24–25
Separating eggs, 14
Storage (of cookies), 30
Sugar, 10

T

Techniques (for baking), 13–15
Time needed (for baking), 5
Tools (for baking), 8–9
 gathering of, 5
 types of, 8–9
 washing of, 7
Turtle bars, 28–29

W

Washing (of hands, ingredients, and tools), 7
Whipping cream, 14